■ SCHOLASTIC

Shoe Box Learning Centers

Counting

by Immacula A. Rhodes

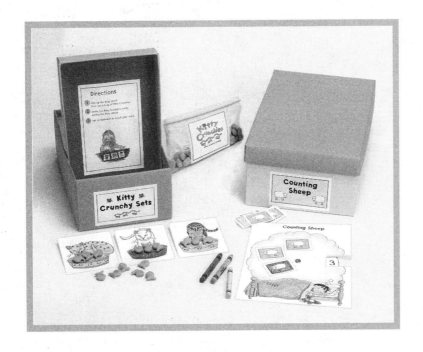

NEW YORK • TORONTO • LONDON • AUCKLAND • SYDNEY
MEXICO CITY • NEW DELHI • HONG KONG • BUENOS AIRES

Teaching *Resources*

To Mom and Dad,
For teaching me the basics of life and encouraging me to pass them on.

"For the Lord is good and his love endures forever; his faithfulness continues through all generations." —Psalm 100:5

Edited by Joan Novelli
Cover design by Maria Lilja
Cover photograph by James Levin/Studio 10
Interior design by Holly Grundon
Interior illustrations by James Graham Hale

ISBN 978-0-545-46867-1

2 3 4 5 6 7 8 9 10   40   19 18 17 16 15 14 13 12

CONTENTS

About This Book

"1, 2, 3, 4, 5,
I caught a fish alive!"

Counting chants, rhymes, and songs have captivated and charmed young children for generations. These number-play ditties are not only fun and engaging but they provide youngsters with meaningful ways to explore, practice, and expand their concept of counting and numbers. Likewise, when you make counting activities in your math center enjoyable and meaningful, children learn essential skills that help build a foundation for future mathematical knowledge.

Shoe Box Learning Centers: Counting makes it easy to set up more than 30 hands-on math centers that playfully engage children in practicing and learning math. Each portable center fits neatly inside a shoe box and can be assembled ahead of time, pulled out as needed, and stored conveniently when not in use. The activities are open-ended, which allows children to repeat the activity as many times as they like, reinforcing learning each time.

The games and activities in *Shoe Box Learning Centers: Counting* are designed for use by small groups of students at centers but can be adapted for whole-class lessons, one-on-one teaching, and independent work. As a supplement to your regular math program, these shoe box learning centers make it simple to weave practice with counting skills and concepts into the following areas throughout the entire school year:

- understanding numbers
- understanding ways of representing numbers and relationships among numbers
- counting with understanding
- skip-counting
- recognizing "how many" in sets of objects
- developing understanding of place value
- connecting number words and numerals to the quantities they represent
- using representations of numerals
- understanding equal groupings of objects
- counting minutes
- counting repeated units to measure objects
- estimating
- counting objects as a computation strategy
- counting days on a calendar
- counting money

Setting Up Shoe Box Learning Centers

Shoe box centers are easy to set up and most materials are either included in this book (as reproducible pages) or are readily available at school or home. For each center in this book, you'll find the following:

- **Label and Directions:** The title of each shoe box center becomes the shoe box label—simply glue it to one end of the shoe box for easy storage and retrieval. Cut out the student directions and glue them to the inside lid of the shoe box.

- **Materials:** Check here to find out which items you'll need for each center.

- **Shoe Box Setup:** Here you'll find simple directions for assembling each center. In most cases, all you'll need to do is gather materials and make copies of the reproducibles.

- **Tips:** These helpful hints include ways to vary and extend the activities.

- **Reproducible Pages:** Record sheets, manipulatives, game boards, and patterns are just some of the shoe box center supplies included in this book. For durability, photocopy pattern pages onto cardstock and/or laminate.

Model each shoe box activity for children before having them try it on their own.

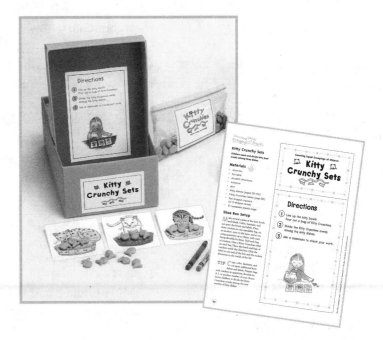

To assemble the centers, photocopy each page on colored paper (or have children decorate), and cut out the title and directions along the lines as indicated. Glue the title to the outside of the box to create a label (on the end or side that will show when you stack and store the shoe boxes). Glue the directions to the inside of the lid. Assemble and prepare any other necessary materials (such as manipulatives and reproducible activity pages), and place these in the box. You may want to enlist parent volunteers to help with this process.

Reinforcing and Assessing Student Learning

To record students' progress as they move through centers, you may want to create assessment files. To do so, provide a pocket folder for each student. In the first pocket, place a copy of the Shoe Box Learning Centers Checklist (see page 7) so that students can keep track of those they have completed. In the second, have students store completed record sheets for you to review. For activities that do not use record sheets, sticky notes work well as an assessment tool. Observe students as they work with a shoe box center and ask related questions. Jot comments on sticky notes, and record the child's name, the date, and the shoe box center name. Keep these on a separate sheet of paper in the pocket folder for easy reference. In addition, comments for any center can be recorded on the checklist. Use these assessments to guide students' work with the centers. Encourage students to revisit those centers where they show a need for more practice.

Meeting the Common Core State Standards

The center activities in this book will help you meet your specific state mathematics standards as well as those recommended by the Common Core State Standards Initiative (CCSSI). Students in grades K–2 are expected to demonstrate increasing awareness and competence in the areas that follow. For more details on these standards, go to the CCSSI Web site: www.corestandards.org.

Counting and Cardinality
Know number names and the count sequence.
> K.CC.1, K.CC.2, K.CC.3

Count to tell the number of objects.
> K.CC.4a, K.CC.4b, K.CC.4, K.CC.5

Compare numbers.
> K.CC.6, K.CC.7

Number and Operations in Base Ten
Work with numbers 11–19 to gain foundations for place value.
> K.NBT.1

Understand place value.
> 1.NBT.2a, 1.NBT.2b, 1.NBT.3
> 2.NBT.1a

Measurement and Data
Describe and compare measurable attributes.
> K.MD.1, K.MD.2

Measure lengths indirectly and by iterating length units.
> 1.MD.2

Measure and estimate lengths in standard units.
> 2.MD.4

Tell and write time.
> 1.MD.3

Work with time and money.
> 2.MD.7

Classify objects and count the number of objects in each category.
> K.MD.3

TIP

To match specific skills and shoe box centers, see the skills matrix on page 8.

Shoe Box Learning Centers Checklist

Name_____

Shoe Box Learning Center	Date	Comments
Counting Sheep		
Confetti Count		
Honeybee Bounce		
Pretty Presents		
Bow-Tie Bears		
Money in the Bank		
Birthday Candle Match		
Clothespin Comparisons		
Nifty Number Line		
Estimation Station		
Around the Shape		
My Town		
Eggs in the Nest		
Shark's Dentist		
Place-Value Stew		
Beanstalks Grow Big		
Fishy Friends		
Space City		
My Crayon Box		
Kitty Crunchy Sets		
Jar Jumpers		
Amber Bear at the Fair		
Long and Tall Dinos		
Ribbons 'n' Rulers		
Fill It Up!		
Penny Weights		
Build a Bean Clock		
Spin a Date		
Candy Shop		
In My Piggy Bank		

Math Skills Matrix

Shoe Box Learning Center

	Number & Operations									
	Recognize how many in sets of objects	Use multiple models to understand place value	Understand position of whole, cardinal, and ordinal numbers	Understand relationships between whole numbers	Understand relationships between number words, numerals, and quantities	Understand various meanings of operations	Understand effects of addition and subtraction	Develop and use strategies for whole number computation	Develop fluency with addition and subtraction number combinations	Use a variety of methods and tools to compute
Counting Sheep	X				X					
Confetti Count	X				X	X	X	X	X	X
Honeybee Bounce			X	X						
Pretty Presents	X				X					
Bow-Tie Bears	X				X		X	X	X	X
Money in the Bank	X				X	X	X	X	X	X
Birthday Candle Match	X				X					
Clothespin Comparisons	X		X	X						
Nifty Number Line	X		X			X	X		X	X
Estimation Station	X		X	X	X				X	X
Around the Shape	X		X	X	X				X	X
My Town	X		X	X	X					
Eggs in the Nest	X				X	X	X	X	X	X
Shark's Dentist	X				X	X	X	X	X	X
Place-Value Stew		X	X	X	X					
Beanstalks Grow Big	X	X			X				X	X
Fishy Friends	X				X					
Space City	X				X					
My Crayon Box	X									
Kitty Crunchy Sets	X			X				X		
Jar Jumpers	X			X	X					
Amber Bear at the Fair	X			X	X					
Long and Tall Dinos	X			X	X					
Ribbons 'n' Rulers	X			X	X				X	X
Fill It Up!	X			X	X				X	X
Penny Weights	X								X	X
Build a Bean Clock	X			X		X	X	X	X	X
Spin a Date	X			X	X				X	X
Candy Shop	X						X	X	X	X
In My Piggy Bank	X				X	X	X	X	X	X

Counting Sheep

Children read numerals and then count sheep to fill a dream bubble.

Materials

- shoe box
- box label
- student directions
- scissors
- glue
- dream-bubble pattern (page 10)
- sheep wheel (page 11)
- sheep cards (page 12)
- paper fasteners

Shoe Box Setup

Copy the dream-bubble pattern, sheep wheel, and sheep cards onto sturdy paper. Color and cut out all the pieces, and laminate for durability. Use the paper fastener to attach the wheel to the back of the dream bubble. Place the dream-bubble wheel and cards inside the shoe box. Glue the label to one end of the box and the student directions to the inside of the lid.

TIP Make this a sensory activity by gluing a bit of cotton on each sheep. As a variation, have children turn the wheel a second time to add more sheep to the bubble. Have children write down both numbers, count the sheep, and tell how many in all.

**Connecting Numerals to the
Quantities They Represent**

Counting Sheep

Directions

① Turn the wheel to a number.

② Count out the same number of sheep. Place the sheep on the dream bubble.

③ Ask a classmate to check your work.

Counting Sheep

Counting Sheep

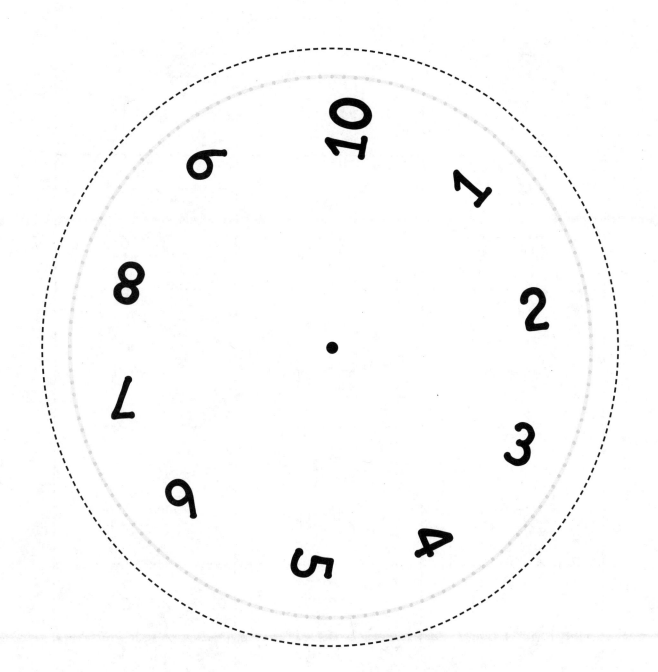

Counting Sheep

Confetti Count

Children decorate a special page with confetti to celebrate counting.

Materials

- shoe box
- box label
- student directions
- scissors
- glue
- Confetti Count page (page 14)
- 2 number cube patterns (page 15)
- assorted "confetti" (such as star stickers, mini-dot stickers, short pieces of curly ribbon, colorful snips of paper, and bits of foil)
- resealable plastic bags

Shoe Box Setup

Make several copies of the confetti-count page. Assemble the number cubes. Place a handful of each type of confetti material in a separate bag. (Restock as necessary.) Place the pages, cubes, bags of confetti, and glue in the shoe box. Glue the label to one end of the box and the student directions to the inside of the lid.

TIP **T**o give children's counting and number recognition skills a workout, make number cubes with higher values. To encourage children to recognize how many in a set or to connect number words to the quantities they represent, use the dotted number and number word cubes (pages 16–17).

Connecting Numerals to the Quantities They Represent

Confetti Count

Directions

① Choose a bag of confetti.

② Roll the number cubes. Count out that number of pieces of confetti and glue (or stick) them to your paper.

③ Repeat steps 1 and 2 three times.

④ Count the number of pieces all together.

Confetti Count

I love to count!

Number Cube

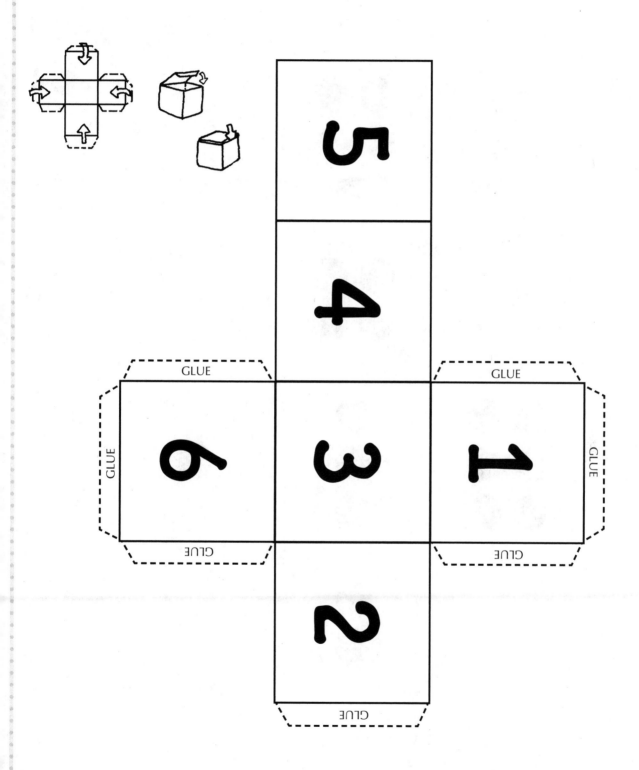

Dotted Number Cube

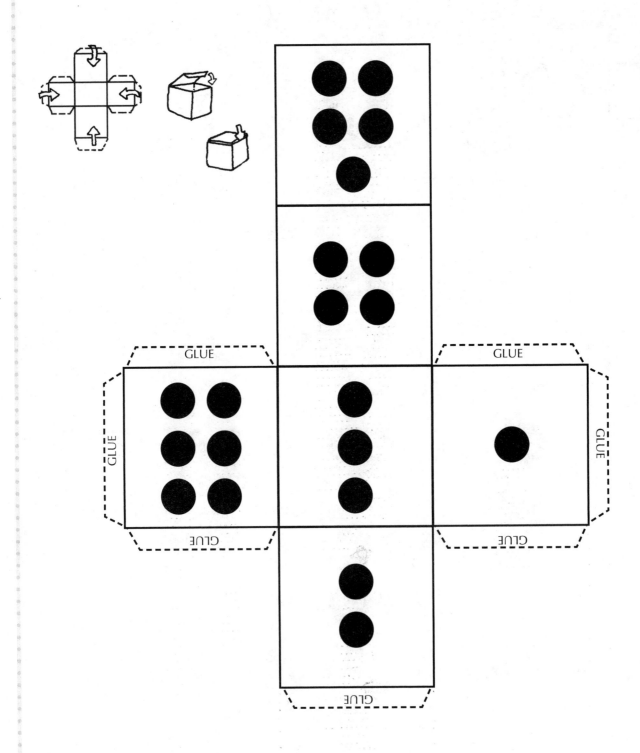

Number Word Cube

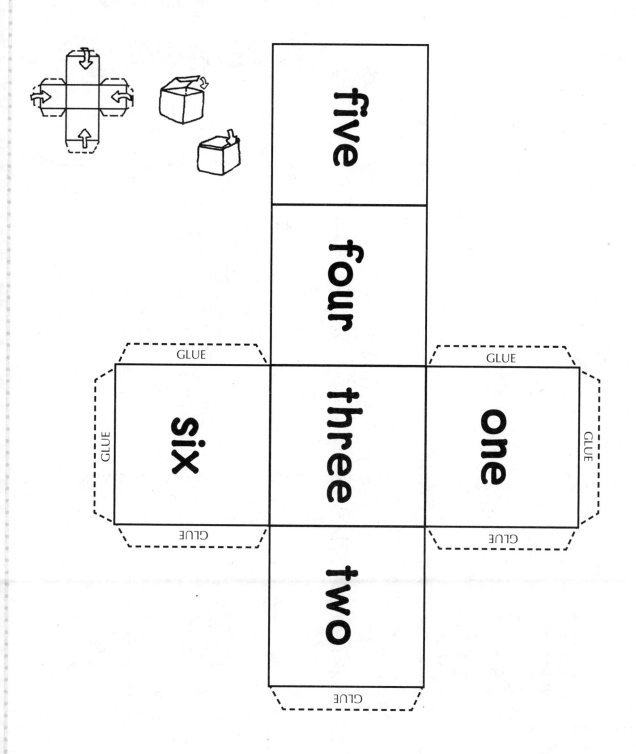

Honeybee Bounce

Children bounce a bee on a beehive to skip-count by 2s, 3s, 4s, 5s, and 10s.

Materials

- shoe box
- box label
- student directions
- scissors
- glue
- game board (page 19)
- honeybee-puppet pattern (page 19)
- crayons or markers
- craft sticks
- 20 or more pennies for each player (each set stored in a resealable bag)

Shoe Box Setup

Copy, color, and cut out five beehive patterns and several honeybees. Write the number 2, 3, 4, 5, or 10 to complete the sentence on each page. Laminate all the pieces. Glue each honeybee to the end of a craft stick to make a stick puppet. Place the beehives, bee puppets, and pennies in the shoe box. Glue the label to one end of the box and the student directions to the inside of the lid.

TIP To practice counting by ones, cut off the sentence under the beehive. Then copy and cut out the pattern and a supply of honeybees. Provide number cubes. Have children roll one or more, count up the total, and place pennies on that number of cells in the beehive. How many rolls does it take to fill up the beehive?

Honeybee Bounce

Directions

① Choose a beehive. Read the sentence under the beehive. This is your counting pattern.

② Place a penny on each beehive cell to show the pattern. Start with the number in the sentence. The penny represents honey.

③ Bounce the bee on each honey-filled cell while you read the number pattern aloud.

Honeybee Bounce Game Board

Fill every 3 cells with honey.

Honeybee Bounce

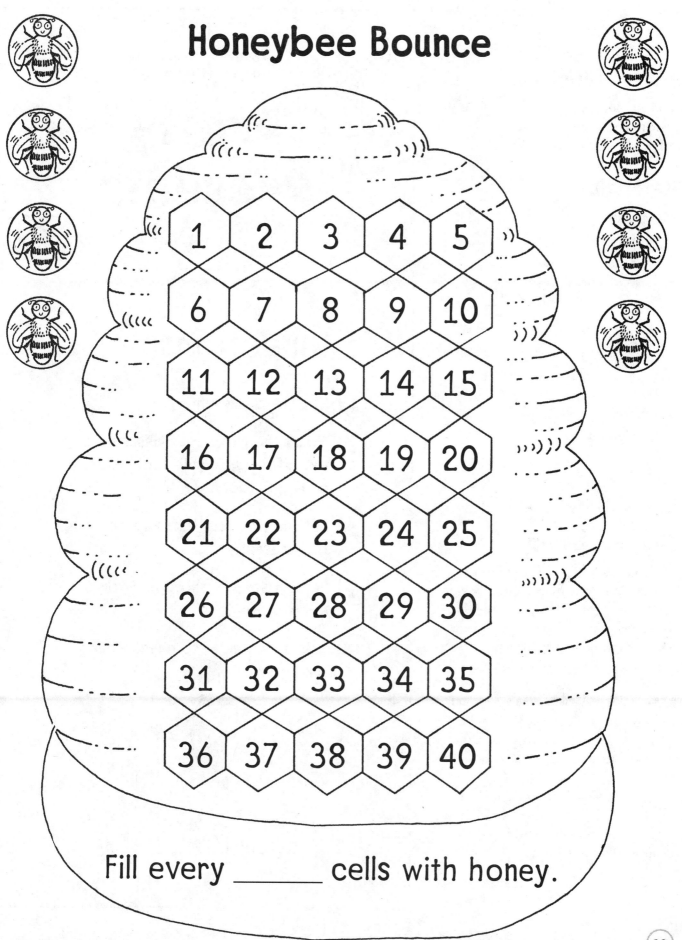

Fill every _____ cells with honey.

Pretty Presents

Children count the designs on pretend presents and write the numbers on gift tags.

Materials

- shoe box
- box label
- student directions
- scissors
- glue
- gift wrap that features repeating pictures that can be counted (such as dogs, stars, or polka dots)
- tagboard
- plain gift tags
- small gift bows
- tape
- wipe-off marker
- paper towels

Shoe Box Setup

For pretend presents, glue sheets of gift wrap (no bigger than the shoe box) to different tagboard shapes. Trim the edges to eliminate any partial pictures. (Include whole shapes only.) Laminate the presents and gift tags. Attach a bow to one end of each gift tag. Place the presents, bows and gift tags, tape, wipe-off marker, and paper towels in the shoebox. Glue the label to one end of the box and the student directions to the inside of the lid.

TIP Copy and cut out different-sized copies of the gift wrap patterns on page 21 to use as templates for the gift wrap.

Recognizing How Many in Sets of Objects

Pretty Presents

Directions

1. Choose a present.

2. Count the number of designs on the gift wrap. Write that number on a gift tag.

3. Set the bow and gift tag on the present.

4. Repeat steps 1 through 3 for each present.

5. Ask a classmate to check your answers.

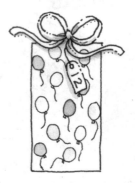

Pretty Presents

Bow-Tie Bears

Children count dots on number cubes, then match the quantity to the corresponding numeral.

Materials

- shoe box
- box label
- student directions
- scissors
- glue
- bear patterns (page 23)
- dotted number cube (page 16)
- several sheets of copy paper in different colors
- bow-tie pasta
- resealable bags

Shoe Box Setup

Copy and laminate several sets of bear patterns, using a different-colored paper for each. Cut along the dashed lines to separate the bears. Place each set of bears in a bag. Make two copies of the dotted number cube and assemble. Place the bears, number cubes, and pasta inside the shoe box. Glue the label to one end of the box and the student directions to the inside of the lid.

TIP To teach number words and the numerals they represent, use the number word cube on page 17. Have children match the number words to the bears labeled 1 through 6.

Recognizing How Many in Sets of Objects

Bow-Tie Bears

Directions
(for 2 or more players)

1. Take out a bag of bears. Arrange the bears in front of you.

2. Roll one cube or both cubes. Count the dots to find out how many there are.

3. Put a bow tie on the bear with the answer. If the bear already has a bow tie, or if there is no matching bear, the next player goes.

4. The first player to place a bow tie on every bear wins the game!

Bow-Tie Bears

Money in the Bank

Children read number words and count out the corresponding number of pennies to place on a piggy bank.

Materials

- shoe box
- box label
- student directions
- scissors
- glue
- piggy bank pattern (page 25)
- number word cube (page 17)
- pennies (about 50; stored in a plastic container)

Shoe Box Setup

Copy and laminate several piggy banks, using different-colored paper for each. Assemble the number word cube. Place the pennies in a container. Place the piggy banks, number cubes, and pennies in the shoe box. Glue the label to one end of the box and the student directions to the inside of the lid.

TIP As children begin to learn about coin values, add nickels and dimes to the coin container. Children can roll the number word cube for each type of coin, and then count the total value of the coins.

Connecting Number Words to the Quantities They Represent

Money in the Bank

Directions
(for 2 or more players)

1. Choose a bank.
   Open the container of pennies.

2. Roll the number word cube.
   Read the word it lands on. Place that number of pennies on your bank.

3. Take turns until every player has had five turns.

4. Count the pennies on your bank. The player with the most pennies wins!

Money in the Bank

Birthday Candle Match

Children use candles on a cake to connect number words and numerals to the quantities they represent.

Materials

* shoe box
* box label
* student directions
* scissors
* glue
* cake pattern (page 27)
* 2 dotted number cubes (page 16)
* large craft sticks (stored in a resealable bag)
* fine-point permanent marker

Shoe Box Setup

Make several copies of the cake pattern on sturdy paper. Color, cut out, and laminate the cakes. Then cut the slits in each one. Write the number word for each numeral from 1 to 12 on a craft stick, creating a set of candles for each player. Assemble two dotted number cubes. Place the cakes, candles, and cubes in the shoe box. Glue the label to one end of the box and the student directions to the inside of the lid.

TIP Invite children to create personal birthday cakes. Have them write the numeral and number word for each candle on their cakes. Display the cakes, grouping those with the same number of candles together.

Understanding Ways of Representing Numbers

Birthday Candle Match

Directions
(for 2 or more players)

1. Choose a birthday cake.

2. Take turns rolling one or both cubes and counting the dots on top.

3. Find the candle with the matching number word. Find the matching number on the cake. Slide the candle into the cake.

4. If a match has already been made for a rolled number, play moves to the next player.

5. The first player to put all the candles on the cake wins.

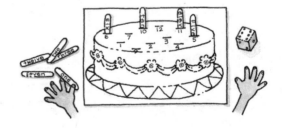

Birthday Candle Match

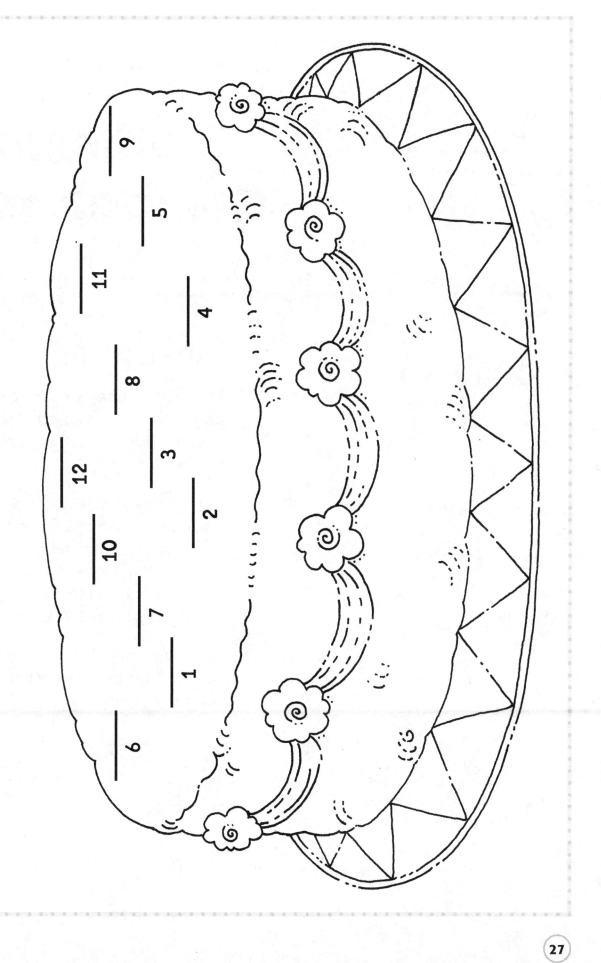

Clothespin Comparisons

Children use clothespins to complete number comparison sentences and develop an understanding of the relationships among numbers.

Materials

- shoe box
- box label
- student directions
- scissors
- glue
- hundred board (page 29)
- paper lunch bag
- record sheet (page 30)
- counters
- clothespin
- pencils

Shoe Box Setup

Copy the hundred board onto sturdy paper and laminate. Cut apart the squares and place them in a paper bag. Make several copies of the record sheet. Place the bag, record sheets, counters, clothespin, and pencils in the shoe box. Glue the label to one end of the box and the student directions to the inside of the lid.

TIP Show children how to use the clothespin to write the number comparison sign on their papers. Simply have them hold the clothespin in place while tracing the inside of the "V" with a pencil.

Understanding "Greater Than" and "Less Than"

Clothespin Comparisons

Directions

1. Take two number squares out of the bag. Place one number in the box on the left. Place the other number in the box on the right.

2. Use the counters to show how many each number equals. Compare the two numbers. Place the clothespin between the two numbers to make the number sentence true. (The wide end always faces the larger number.)

3. Write the number sentence on your paper. Then put the number squares back in the bag.

4. Repeat steps 1 through 3 for each row on your paper.

Clothespin Comparisons

Hundred Board

1	2	3	4	5	6	7	8	9	10
11	12	13	14	15	16	17	18	19	20
21	22	23	24	25	26	27	28	29	30
31	32	33	34	35	36	37	38	39	40
41	42	43	44	45	46	47	48	49	50
51	52	53	54	55	56	57	58	59	60
61	62	63	64	65	66	67	68	69	70
71	72	73	74	75	76	77	78	79	80
81	82	83	84	85	86	87	88	89	90
91	92	93	94	95	96	97	98	99	100

Clothespin Comparisons

Key

is less than   is greater than

Nifty Number Line

Children develop an understanding of the relative position of whole numbers by naming objects by their ordinal position on a number line.

Materials

- shoe box
- box label
- student directions
- scissors
- glue
- number line and number cards (page 32)
- 25 or more small objects (such as counters, toy animals, and coins); store in a resealable bag
- paper lunch bags

Shoe Box Setup

Make several copies of the number line patterns and cards. Cut out the number line patterns and glue each one together where indicated. Cut apart the number cards. Laminate all the pieces. Place each set of number cards in a paper bag and the objects in a resealable bag. Place the number lines, bag of cards, and objects in the shoe box. Glue the label to one end of the box and the student directions to the inside of the lid.

TIP Apply the same concept of this shoe box center to a movement game. Have children line up along a length of rope. Give a command, such as "Hop three times" or "Count to 10." Then call a child by his or her ordinal position (first, second, tenth) to perform the action.

Understanding Ordinal Numbers

Nifty Number Line

5 6 7 8

Directions

(for 2 or more players)

1. Choose a number line. Count out ten different objects. Place each object in a box on the number line.

2. Choose a card from the bag and read it. Count up to the object in that position on your number line. Take that object off the number line. Place the card back in the bag.

3. If the object in that position has already been removed, the next player takes a turn.

4. The first player to empty his or her number line wins!

Nifty Number Line

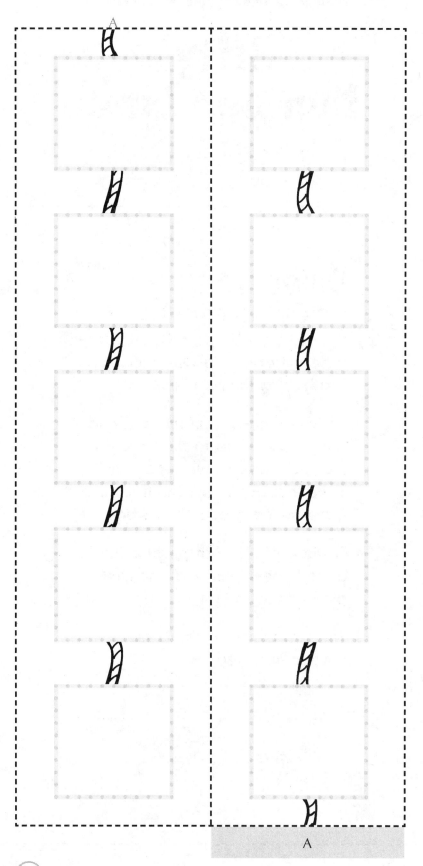

5th fifth	10th tenth
4th fourth	9th ninth
3rd third	8th eighth
2nd second	7th seventh
1st first	6th sixth

Estimating and Counting

Estimation Station

Children estimate and count objects in a jar.

Materials

- shoe box
- box label
- student directions
- scissors
- glue
- hundred board (page 34)
- clear plastic jar with lid (such as a peanut butter jar)
- 100 bear counters, pasta shells, plastic soda bottle lids, or other items that can be used for counting (stored in a resealable bag)
- crayons

Shoe Box Setup

Make several copies of the hundred board. Fill a jar with up to 100 objects and secure the lid. Place the hundred boards, jar, and crayons in the shoe box. Glue the label to one end of the box and the student directions to the inside of the lid.

TIP Cut the hundred board into ten rows. Have children arrange the rows in order to reassemble the board. For a greater challenge, cut each row in half to make number strips of five squares each. Then have students reassemble the board.

Estimating and Counting

Estimation Station

Directions

① Guess how many objects are in the jar. Write that number at the top of the hundred board. Make an X in that number of squares.

② Count the objects in the jar. Write that number at the top of the hundred board and circle it. Color that number of squares.

③ Check to see if your estimate was more than, less than, or the same as the number of objects in the jar.

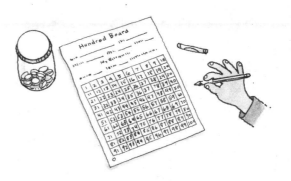

Estimation Station

Name_____ Date_____

How many objects?

My guess _____ The actual number _____

My estimate was:

more than _____ less than _____ the same as _____
the number of objects.

1	2	3	4	5	6	7	8	9	10
11	12	13	14	15	16	17	18	19	20
21	22	23	24	25	26	27	28	29	30
31	32	33	34	35	36	37	38	39	40
41	42	43	44	45	46	47	48	49	50
51	52	53	54	55	56	57	58	59	60
61	62	63	64	65	66	67	68	69	70
71	72	73	74	75	76	77	78	79	80
81	82	83	84	85	86	87	88	89	90
91	92	93	94	95	96	97	98	99	100

Around the Shape

Children estimate and count how many clothespins fit around a shape.

Materials

- shoe box
- box label
- student directions
- scissors
- glue
- shape patterns (page 36)
- posterboard
- 50 spring-close clothespins (stored in a resealable bag)
- paper
- pencils

Shoe Box Setup

Using the shape patterns as templates, trace each one onto a sheet of posterboard. Cut out and laminate the shapes. Place the shapes, clothespins, paper, and pencils in the shoe box. Glue the label to one end of the box and the student directions to the inside of the lid.

TIP To simplify counting the clothespins and to reinforce number sequence, label each clothespin with a number, starting with 1. Have children put the clothespins on the shape in numerical order. The last clothespin they clip to each shape will show the total number of clothespins used.

Estimating and Counting

Around the Shape

Directions

1. Choose a shape.

2. Estimate how many clothespins will fit around the shape. Write your guess on a sheet of paper.

3. Clip clothespins around the shape. Count the clothespins. Write this number next to your guess. How close was your guess?

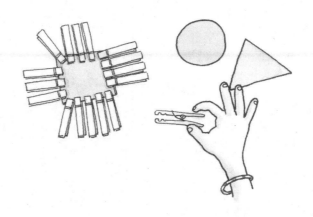

Around the Shape

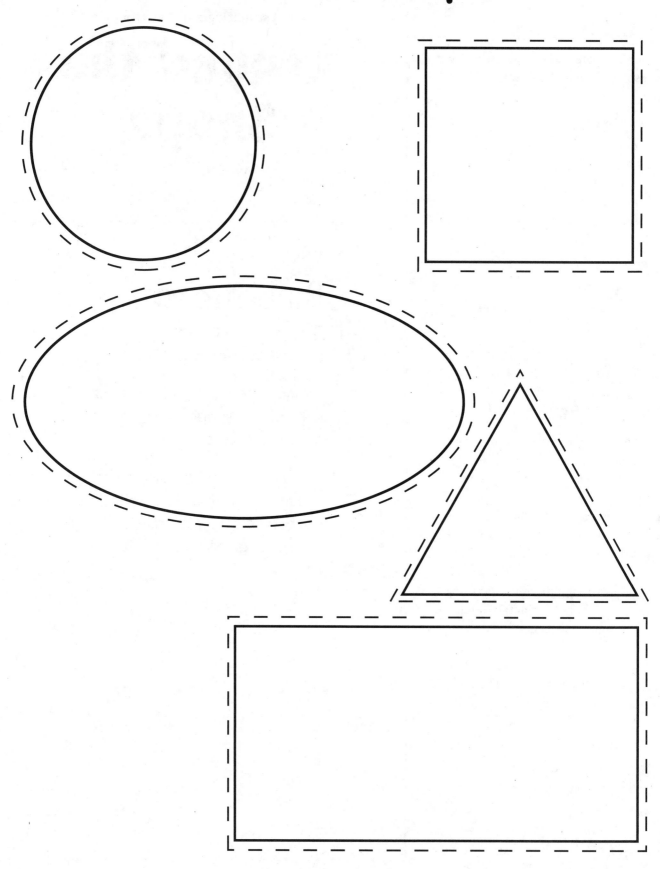

My Town

Children sequence models of their hometown buildings by counting the number of blocks used to construct each one.

Materials

- shoe box
- box label
- student directions
- scissors
- glue
- small interlocking blocks (stored in a large resealable bag)
- small sticky notes
- pencils

Shoe Box Setup

Place the blocks, sticky notes, and pencils in the shoe box. Glue the label to one end of the box and the student directions to the inside of the lid.

TIP **A**s a variation, invite children to use only blocks of the same color to construct each building, so that there is a different structure for each color. After all the blocks have been used, have students compare the number of blocks in each structure. Ask them to name the structures by color in order from most to fewest.

Counting and Sequencing

My Town

Directions

(1) Use the blocks to make models of some buildings where you live.

(2) Count the number of blocks in each building.

(3) Write the numbers on sticky notes and attach them to the buildings.

(4) Place the buildings in order from the most to the fewest blocks.

Eggs in the Nest

Children count dots on an egg to find the sum of two numbers.

Materials

- shoe box
- box label
- student directions
- scissors
- glue
- record sheet and egg cards (page 39)
- paper lunch bag
- brown crinkle-cut paper strips
- small plastic eggs
- pencils

Shoe Box Setup

Cut out several copies of the record sheet and the egg cards. Place an egg card in each plastic egg. Roll down the top of the paper bag to create a nest about two inches tall. Line the nest with crinkle-cut paper strips. Place the eggs in the nest. Place the record sheets, egg-filled nest, and pencils in the shoe box. Glue the label to one end of the box and the student directions to the inside of the lid.

TIP Prepare several sets of eggs with egg cards in them. Distribute the eggs to students. Then call out a sum from 1 to 18. Challenge children to work together to find as many number pairs as possible that equal the given sum.

Counting Up

Eggs in the Nest

Directions

(1) Choose two eggs. Open each one and read the number. Write the number for each egg in a number sentence.

(2) Draw dots on an egg for each number. Draw them on the egg picture next to your number sentence.

(3) Count the dots. Write the total number of dots in the number sentence.

(4) Repeat for each egg picture on your paper.

Eggs in the Nest

Name _____ Date _____

___ + ___ = ___

___ + ___ = ___

___ + ___ = ___

___ + ___ = ___

0	1	2	3	4
5	6	7	8	9

Shark's Dentist

Children pull teeth from a shark's mouth to practice counting back.

Materials

- shoe box
- box label
- student directions
- scissors
- glue
- game board and shark teeth (page 41)
- white craft foam
- tape
- resealable plastic bags
- dotted number cube pattern (page 16)
- pencils
- paper

Shoe Box Setup

Color, cut out, and laminate several copies of the game board and shark teeth. Using rolled pieces of tape (or glue), attach the shark teeth to craft foam. Cut through all thicknesses to separate the teeth. Place each set of 20 teeth in a bag. Assemble the number cube. Place the game boards, teeth, number cube, pencils, and paper in the shoe box. Glue the label to one end of the box and the student directions to the inside of the lid.

TIP Use teeth cut from different colors of craft foam to make up number stories for children to solve. For example, "The shark dentist pulled three blue teeth and two red teeth. How many teeth are left?"

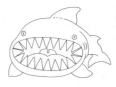

Counting Back

Shark's Dentist

Directions

① Choose a shark game board. Fill the shark's mouth with teeth. Count the teeth. Write the number on a sheet of paper.

② Roll the number cube. "Pull" that many teeth from the shark's mouth. Write a number sentence to show how many teeth are left.

③ Roll the cube again. Pull that many teeth from the shark's mouth. On a sheet of paper, write a number sentence to show how many teeth are left.

④ Continue rolling the number cube and pulling teeth. Write number sentences to show how many are left.

Shark's Dentist

Place-Value Stew

Children fill in a place-value chart as they count vegetables to add to a pot of stew.

Materials

- shoe box
- box label
- student directions
- scissors
- glue
- record sheet (page 43)
- number board (page 44)
- pennies
- pencils

Shoe Box Setup

Make several copies of the record sheet and number board. Place the record sheets, number boards, pennies, and pencils in the shoe box. Glue the label to one end of the box and the student directions to the inside of the lid.

TIP Bring in a recipe for vegetable stew. Invite children to help chop the vegetables for the recipe. Then have them count the number of pieces for each vegetable before adding them to the stew.

Developing Place-Value Concepts

Place-Value Stew

Directions

① Toss a penny onto the number board. Write that number in the "Hundreds" place next to the carrot (on your pot of stew).

② Toss the penny again. Write this number in the "Tens" place. Toss the penny again. Write the number in the "Ones" place.

③ Repeat to fill in the numbers for potatoes. Do the same for beans, tomatoes, corn, onions, and celery.

④ Write the total number for each ingredient. This shows how many pieces of each are in your stew.

⑤ Compare the numbers. Circle the ingredient with the most pieces. Draw an X on the one with the fewest.

Place-Value Stew

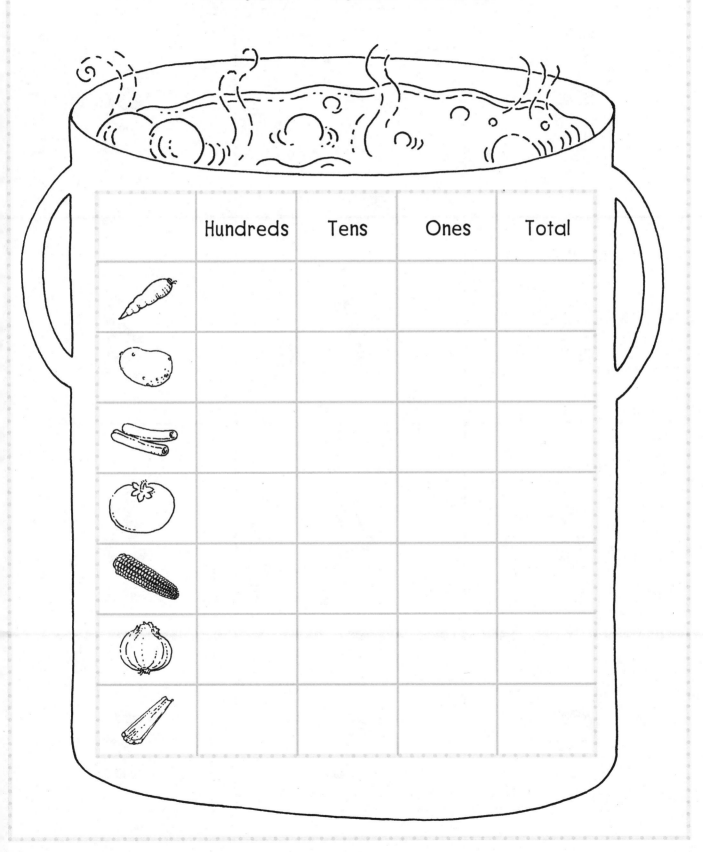

	Hundreds	Tens	Ones	Total

Place-Value Stew
Number Board

0	1	2
6	7	8
3	4	5
9	1	2

Beanstalks Grow Big

Children build numbers by rolling a number cube, counting beans, and placing them on beanstalk place-value holders.

Materials

- shoe box
- box label
- student directions
- scissors
- glue
- number cube pattern (page 15)
- beanstalk mat (page 46)
- dried beans (stored in a resealable bag)
- paper
- pencils

Shoe Box Setup

Make copies of the beanstalk mat. Copy and assemble the number cube. Place the beanstalk mats, number cube, beans, paper, and pencils in the shoe box. Glue the label to one end of the box and the student directions to the inside of the lid.

TIP To make larger numbers, have children use two (or more) number cubes. Add more beans to the shoe box.

Understanding Place-Value Concepts

Beanstalks Grow Big

Directions
(for 2 or more players)

1. Place a beanstalk mat in front of you.

2. Take turns rolling the cube 20 times. On each roll, place that number of beans on the "Ones" beanstalk.

3. When you get 10 beans on the "Ones" beanstalk, take them off and place 1 bean on the "Tens" beanstalk.

4. When you get 10 beans on the "Tens" beanstalk, take them off and place 1 bean on the "Hundreds" beanstalk.

5. At the end of the game, use the beans and beanstalks to help find your total bean count. Write that number on a sheet of paper. The player with the highest number wins.

Beanstalks Grow Big

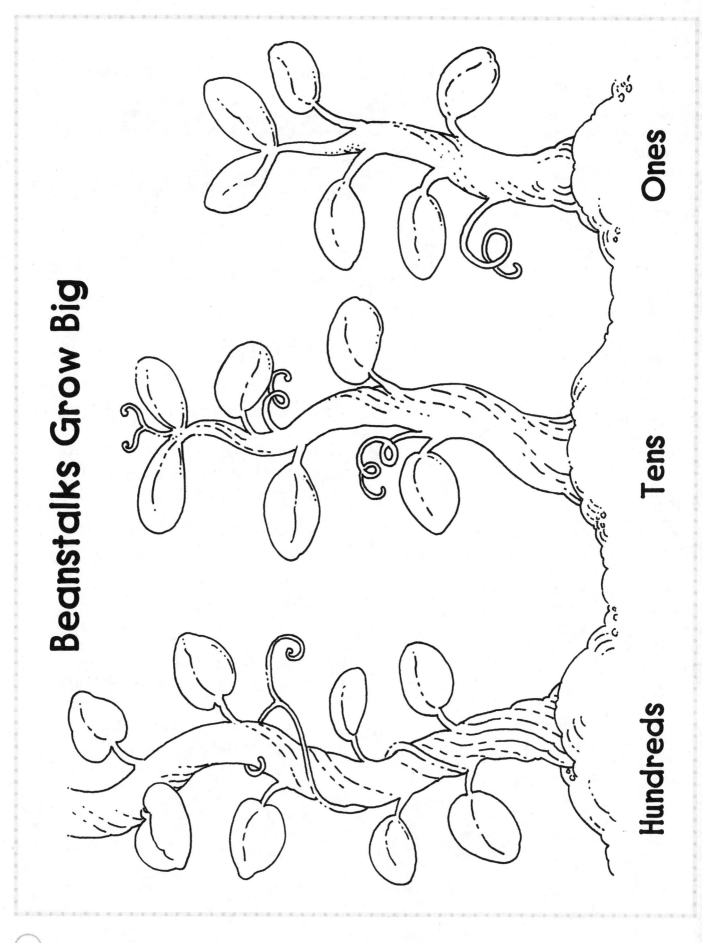

Ones

Tens

Hundreds

Fishy Friends

Children count and follow directions to put fish in the fish tank.

Materials

- shoe box
- box label
- student directions
- scissors
- glue
- fish tank (page 48)
- game board and fish cards (page 49)
- number cube pattern (page 15)
- wipe-off markers
- paper towels

Shoe Box Setup

Copy the fish tank, game board, and fish cards onto sturdy paper for each player. Color, cut out, and laminate all the pieces. Then cut along the dotted lines around the shell and door on each tank. Assemble the number cube. Place the fish tanks, game boards, fish cards, number cube, wipe-off markers, and paper towels in the shoe box. Glue the label to one end of the box and the student directions to the inside of the lid.

TIP For a fun movement activity, invite children to pretend they are a school of fish in their own fish tank—the classroom! Have them follow directions to "swim" in, out, through, under, over, and around various objects. Use as many directional and positional words as possible to reinforce spatial concepts.

Counting and Following Directions

Fishy Friends

Directions
(for 2 or more players)

① Each player chooses a fish tank, game board, and set of six fish cards.

② Take turns rolling the number cube onto your game board. Read the box the cube lands on.

③ Follow the directions to place that many fish in the fish tank. Then draw an X on the used box on your game board. Use your fish cards for each turn.

④ If the cube lands on a box with an X, the next player goes.

⑤ The first player to mark an X on all the boxes wins.

Fishy Friends

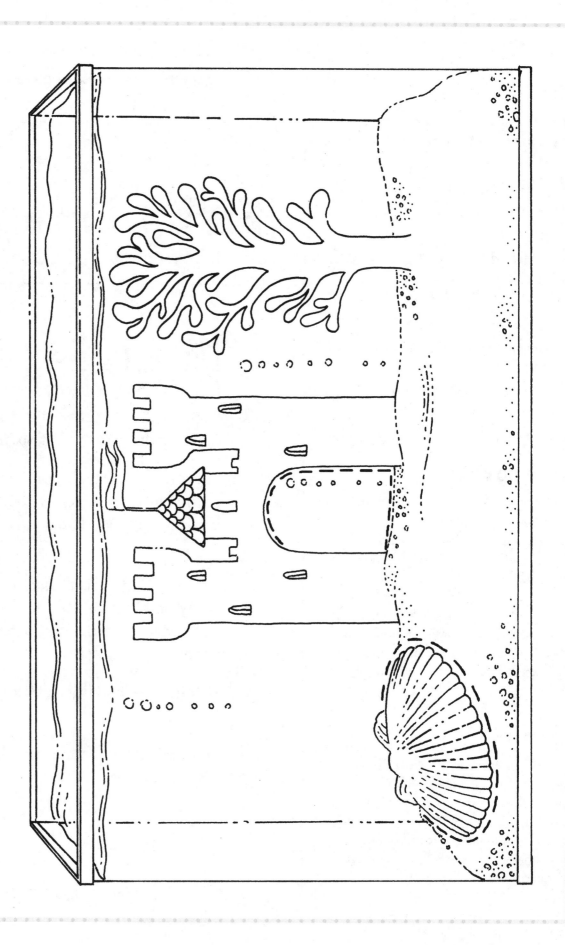

Fishy Friends
Game Board

in front of 	through	at the bottom of
under	in the middle of	next to
at the top of 	above 	behind 

Fish Cards

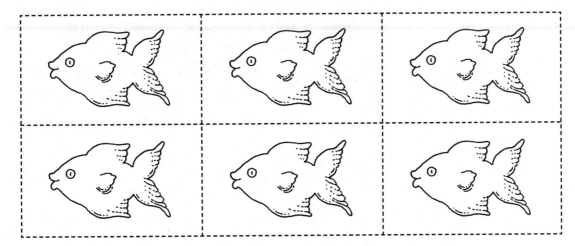

Space City

Children find and count matching shapes in Space City.

Materials

- shoe box
- box label
- student directions
- scissors
- glue
- Space City scene (page 51)
- crayons
- drawing paper

Shoe Box Setup

Make several copies of the Space City scene. Place the scenes, crayons, and paper in the shoe box. Glue the label to one end of the box and the student directions to the inside of the lid.

TIP Invite children to use the same shapes to create other pictures—for example, a shape pet, a shape person, or a shape vehicle. They can add details to complete the scene.

Recognizing and Counting Shapes

Space City

Directions

1. Choose one of the shapes in the Space City picture.

2. Find all the matching shapes in the picture and count them. The shapes do not need to be the same size.

3. Write your answer in the same shape at the bottom of your paper.

4. Do the same for each other shape. Then color the picture.

5. Use the same shapes to draw a new shape city. Count the number of each shape in the new picture. Write the number of each shape on your paper.

Space City

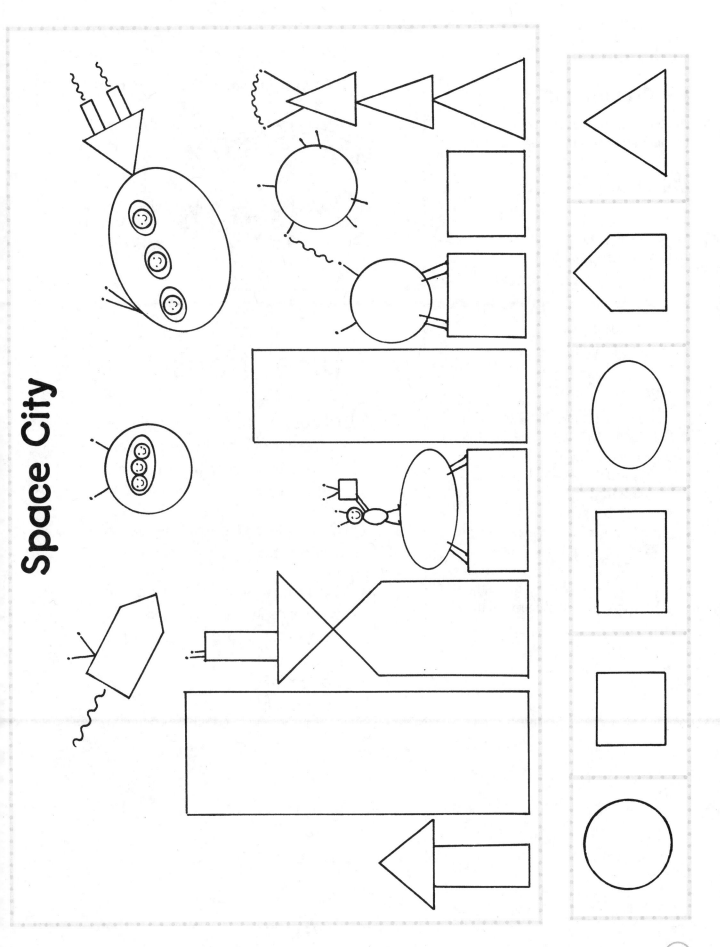

My Crayon Box

Children create a crayon pattern and count the number of crayons for each color.

Materials

- shoe box
- box label
- student directions
- scissors
- glue
- record sheet (page 53)
- crayons in different colors

Shoe Box Setup

Make several copies of the record sheet. Place the record sheets and crayons in the shoe box. Glue the label to one end of the box and the student directions to the inside of the lid.

TIP For a fun variation, place five crayons in each color (5 red, 5 blue, 5 green, and so on) in the shoe box. Invite children to use the actual crayons to create patterns on their crayon boxes.

Recognizing and Extending Patterns

My Crayon Box

Directions

① Choose up to three crayons in different colors. For each color, fill in a crayon at the bottom of the page.

② Color the crayons in the box to make a pattern.

③ Count how many crayons of each color are in the box. Write the number next to the matching crayon at the bottom of the paper.

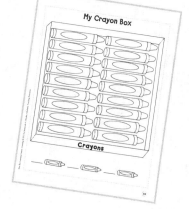

My Crayon Box

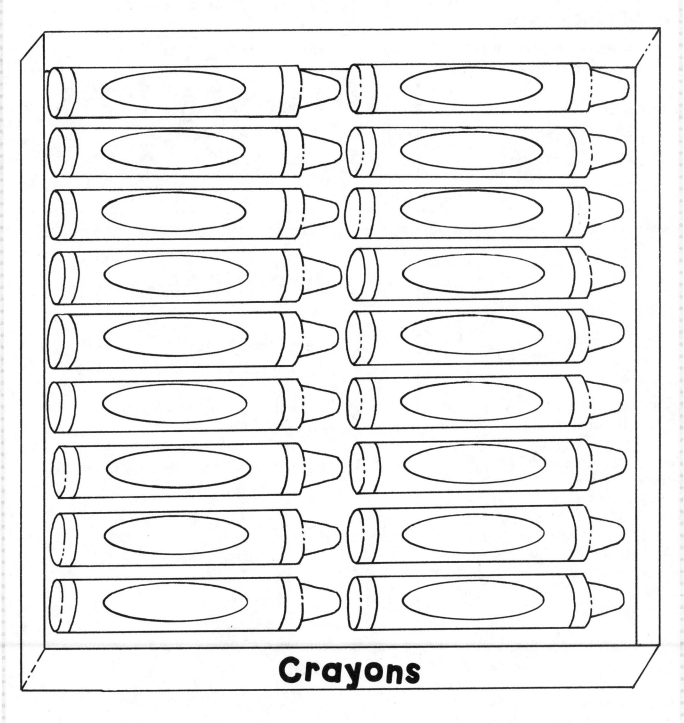

Crayons

___ ___ ___

Kitty Crunchy Sets

Children count and divide kitty food evenly among three dishes.

Materials

- shoe box
- box label
- student directions
- scissors
- glue
- kitty dishes (pages 55–56)
- Kitty Crunchies labels (page 56)
- fish-shaped crackers (or O-shaped cereal)
- 10 resealable plastic bags

Shoe Box Setup

Make several copies of the kitty bowls and labels. Color, laminate, and cut apart the bowls and labels. Place three crackers in one resealable bag, six in another, nine in the next, and so on, using quantities up to thirty, with each being divisible by three. Seal each bag of crackers. Glue a Kitty Crunchies label on each bag. Place the bowls and bags of crackers inside the shoe box. Glue the label to one end of the box and the student directions to the inside of the lid.

TIP Copy, color, laminate, and cut apart additional kitty dishes and labels. Prepare bags with crackers in quantities divisible by 4, 5, or another number of your choice. Invite children to divide the Kitty Crunchies evenly among the new number of kitty dishes.

Counting Equal Groupings of Objects
Kitty Crunchy Sets

Directions

1. Line up the kitty bowls. Pour out a bag of Kitty Crunchies.

2. Divide the Kitty Crunchies evenly among the kitty dishes.

3. Ask a classmate to check your work.

Kitty Crunchy Sets

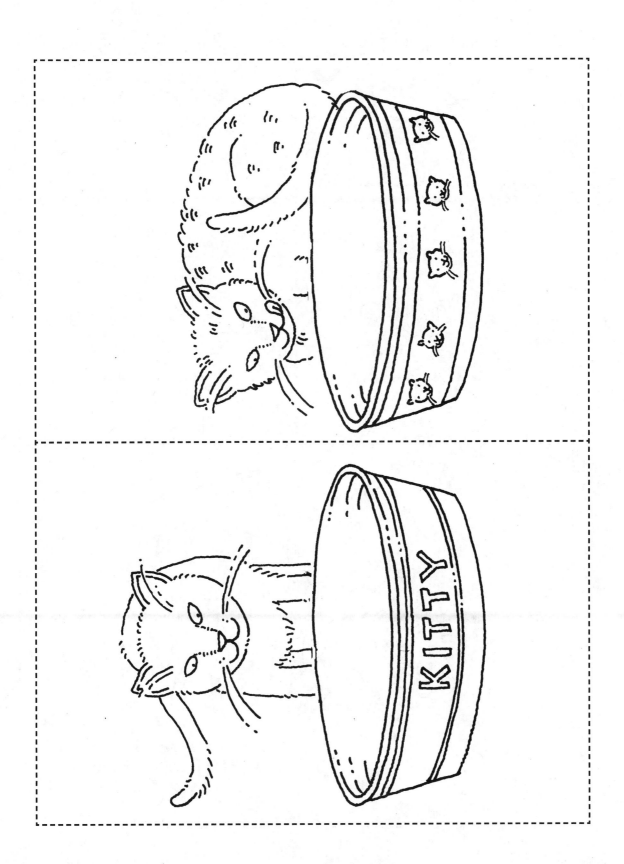

Kitty Crunchy Sets

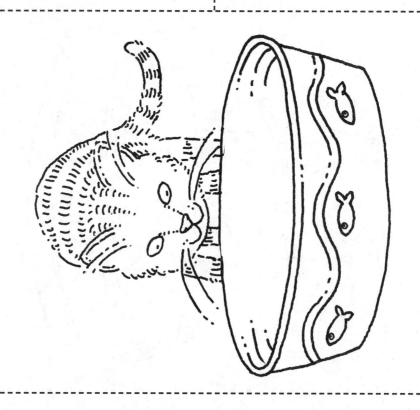

Jar Jumpers

Children count and sort crickets into jars according to how they are dressed.

Materials

- shoe box
- box label
- student directions
- scissors
- glue
- jar patterns (page 58)
- cricket cards (page 59)
- paper bag
- number cube pattern (page 15)

Shoe Box Setup

Make copies of the jar pattern and cut them apart. Glue bow ties, sunglasses, and hats on the jar lids (one per lid). Make five to ten copies of the cricket cards and cut them apart. Place the cards in the paper bag. Copy and assemble the number cube. Place the jars, cards, and number cube in the shoe box. Glue the label to one end of the box and the student directions to the inside of the lid.

TIP Invite children to squat on the floor and pretend to be crickets. Then call out an article of clothing, hair color, beginning letter of a name, or any other attribute related to students. Children who fit that category jump into the air and land standing. The class counts to see how many children belong to that category. Everyone goes back into cricket position to play again.

Counting and Classifying

Jar Jumpers

Directions
(for 2 or more players)

① Each player takes eight cricket cards from the bag and one set of jars (bow tie, sunglasses, hats).

② To Play: Roll the number cube. Look at your cards to see if you have that number of crickets that are dressed alike. If you do, jump the crickets onto the matching jar. Then take the same number of cards from the bag. If you do not have enough cards, the next player takes a turn.

③ Continue taking turns. The first player to jump all of his or her crickets into the jars wins.

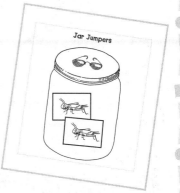

Jar Jumpers

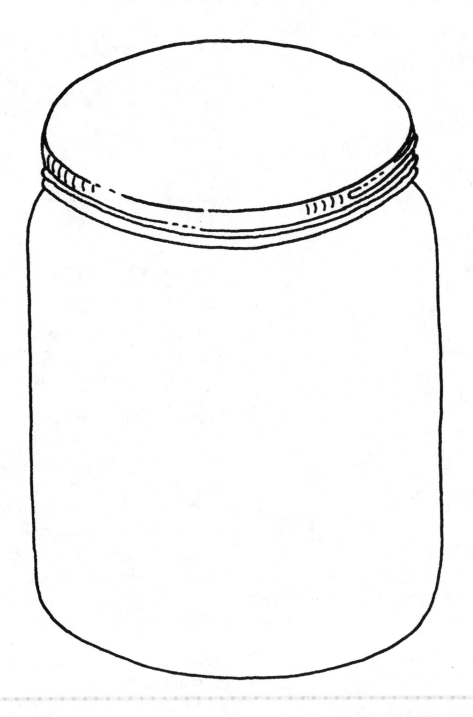

Jar Jumpers

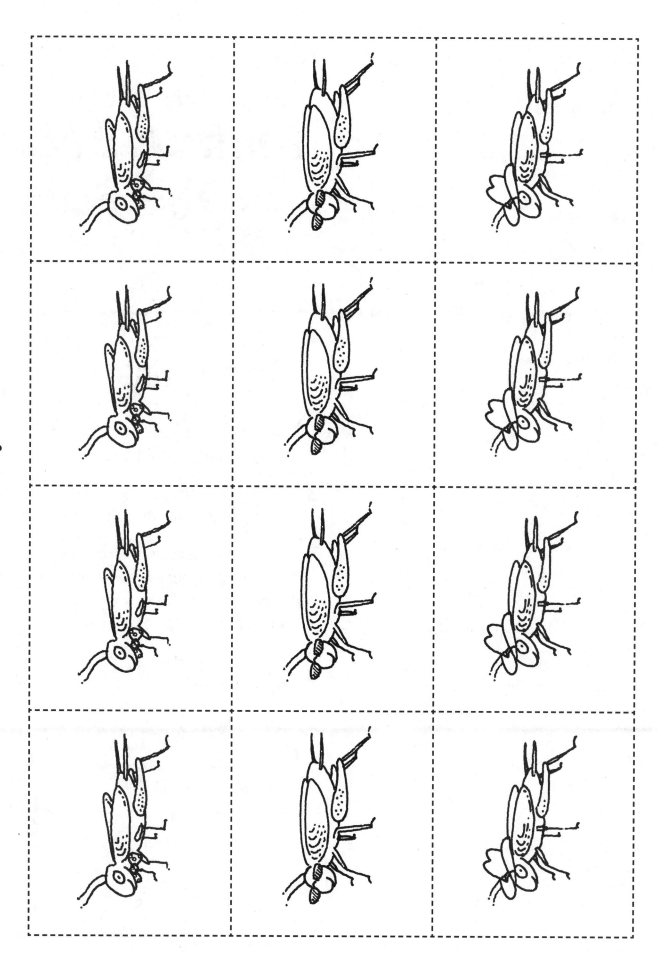

Amber Bear at the Fair

Children measure and count units to find the distance to each of Amber Bear's favorite fair sites.

Materials

- shoe box
- box label
- student directions
- scissors
- glue
- fair map (page 61)
- counters (such as pom-poms, dried beans, hole reinforcers, or any other small, easy-to-count objects, stored in resealable bags)
- paper
- pencils
- crayons

Shoe Box Setup

Make several copies of the fair map. Place the maps, counters, and crayons in the shoe box. Glue the label to one end of the box and the student directions to the inside of the lid.

TIP Invite children to use larger units of nonstandard measure, such as blocks or unsharpened pencils, to measure the distance between the classroom door and teacher's desk, the reading and art centers, and other locations in the classroom.

Counting Repeated Units to Measure

Amber Bear at the Fair

Directions

1. Choose a place at the fair for Amber Bear to visit.

2. Place a counter on Start. Place more counters end to end along the path.

3. Count the number of units it takes to reach the place. Draw a picture of your counter. On a sheet of paper, write how many you counted.

4. Repeat steps 1 to 3, using other counters.

5. Color the picture. Share your findings with a classmate.

Amber Bear at the Fair

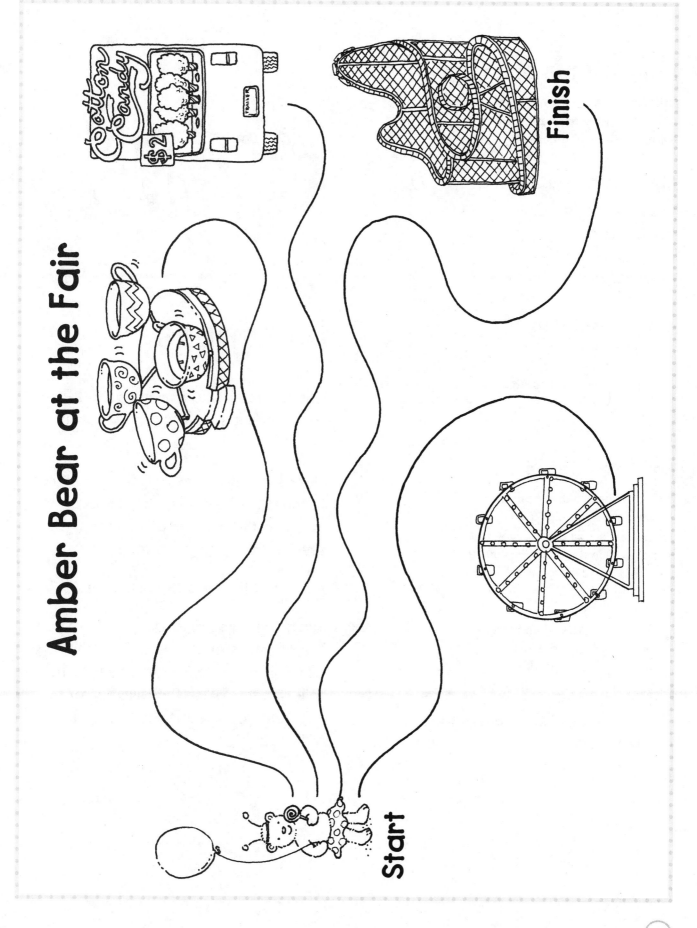

Finish

Start

Long and Tall Dinos

Children repeat and count nonstandard units of measure to find the length and height of different dinosaurs.

Materials

- shoe box
- box label
- student directions
- scissors
- glue
- dinosaur cards (page 63)
- counters (such as dried beans, small pom-poms, or uncooked popcorn, stored in resealable bags)
- pencils
- crayons

Shoe Box Setup

Enlarge and make several copies of the dinosaur cards. Cut apart the cards. Place the dinosaur cards, counters, pencils, and crayons in the shoe box. Glue the label to one end of the box and the student directions to the inside of the lid.

TIP Ask children to sequence their dinosaurs by height, starting with the shortest. Then have them sequence the dinosaurs by length, starting with the shortest. Explain that *short* can be used to describe both height and length.

Counting Repeated
Units to Measure

Long and Tall Dinos

Directions

1 Choose four dinosaur cards and a set of counters. Color the dinosaur cards.

2 Choose a dinosaur. Use the counters to measure how long the dinosaur is. Write the number of counters you used in the "____ units long" space.

3 Repeat with the other dinosaurs.

4 Using the same dinosaur cards, place the counters end to end from the bottom of one dinosaur's feet to its tallest part. Write that number of counters you used in the "____ units tall" space.

Long and Tall Dinos

_____ units long
_____ units tall

_____ units long
_____ units tall

_____ units long
_____ units tall

_____ units long
_____ units tall

_____ units long
_____ units tall

Ribbons 'n' Rulers

Children use a ruler to measure and find the difference between two lengths of ribbon.

Materials

- shoe box
- box label
- student directions
- scissors
- glue
- assorted ribbons cut into 1- to 8-inch lengths
- paper
- tape
- inch ruler
- pencil

Shoe Box Setup

Place the ribbons, paper, tape, ruler, and pencil in the shoe box. Glue the label to one end of the shoe box and the student directions to the inside of the lid.

TIP If desired, replace the inch ruler with a centimeter ruler, and then cut ribbons into one-centimeter increments.

Counting Standard Units to Compare Objects

Ribbons 'n' Rulers

Directions

1. Choose two ribbons. Tape the end of each one to the left edge of your paper.

2. Measure the ribbons with a ruler. Make a mark for each inch under the ribbon. Then write the measurement in inches.

3. Count the number of inches between the longest and shortest ribbon.

4. Share your answer with a classmate.

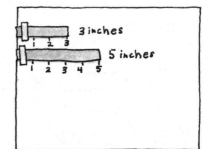

Fill It Up!

Children compare the volume of containers by counting spoonfuls of rice into each.

Materials

- shoe box
- box label
- student directions
- scissors
- glue
- unbreakable containers of various shapes and sizes (such as small chip canisters, plastic or paper cups, and snack-size cups)
- uncooked rice (in a container with a lid)
- measuring spoons
- sticky notes
- pencils

Shoe Box Setup

Place the containers, rice, spoons, sticky notes, and pencils in the shoe box. Glue the label to one end of the box and the student directions to the inside of the lid.

TIP As an alternative, add a different material, such as dried beans or macaroni, to the shoe box. Have children measure one substance into a container, empty it, and then measure the second substance into the same container. Ask them to compare their results.

Using Tally Marks to Count

Fill It Up!

Directions

(1) Choose two containers. Put a sticky note next to each one.

(2) Fill each container with one spoonful of rice at a time. Make a tally mark for each spoonful of rice you add.

(3) Count and write the number of spoonfuls needed to fill each container.

(4) Compare the numbers to see which container has the greatest volume (holds the most).

Penny Weights

Children count how many pennies it takes to balance various objects on a scale.

Materials

- shoe box
- box label
- student directions
- scissors
- glue
- record sheets (page 67)
- small, lightweight objects (such as crayons, clothespins, craft sticks, pencils, and paintbrushes; 2–4 of each)
- pennies (stored in a resealable bag)
- crayons
- balance scale

Shoe Box Setup

Make several copies of the record sheets and cut them apart. Place the record sheets, objects, pennies, and crayons in the shoe box. Set up the balance scale at the center. Glue the label to one end of the box and the student directions to the inside of the lid.

TIP Invite children to balance the scales with other items, such as paper clips, dried beans, and pasta wheels. Have them compare their results with those from the penny weights.

Using Tally Marks to Count

Penny Weights

Directions

1. Choose a few of the same kinds of objects. Place them on one side of the scale. Draw them on the scale on your paper.

2. Add pennies to the other side of the scale until it balances. Write tally marks for the pennies as you go along.

3. Count the tally marks.

4. Tell a classmate how many pennies the objects weigh.

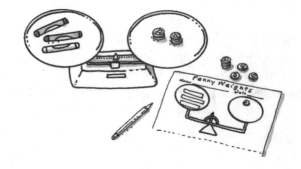

Penny Weights

Name _____ Date _____

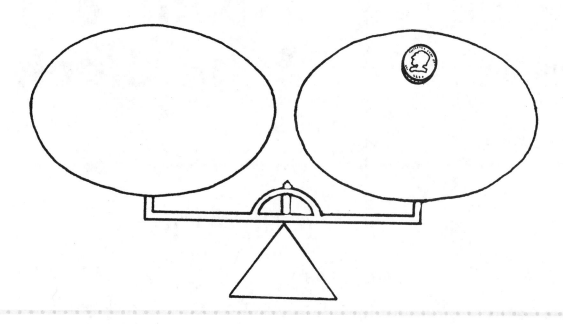

Penny Weights

Name _____ Date _____

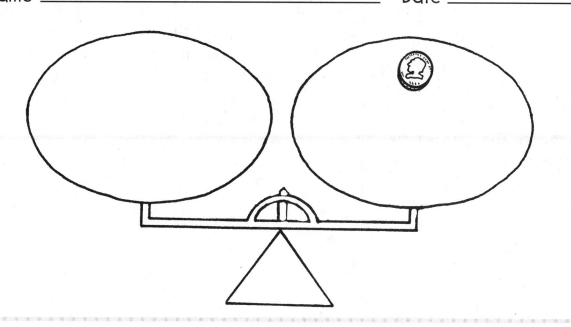

Build a Bean Clock

Children count around this unique bean clock to practice telling time in five-minute increments.

Materials

- shoe box
- box label
- student directions
- scissors
- glue
- clock pattern (page 69)
- large dried beans, such as limas (stored in a resealable bag)
- paper fasteners

Shoe Box Setup

Make several sturdy copies of the clock and clock hands. Cut out and laminate all the pieces. Use a paper fastener to attach each set of clock hands to a clock. Place the clocks and beans in the shoe box. Glue the box label to one end of the box and the student directions to the inside of the lid.

TIP **E**xtend learning to include counting by ones by giving children small beans to place on each line between the clock numbers. Challenge children to use their clocks to practice telling time to the minute. To do this, have them count large beans starting at 1 up to the large bean just before the minute hand. Then have them count small beans by ones to the minute hand.

Counting Minutes

Build a Bean Clock

Directions
(for 2 players)

1. Each player takes a clock. Place a bean on the circle next to each number.

2. Ask your partner to set the clock by pointing the hour and minute hands to different beans on the clock.

3. Tell the time. To find the hour, name the number that the hour hand points to. To find the minutes, skip-count the beans by fives, starting at 1 and stopping at the bean that the minute hand points to.

Build a Bean Clock

Build a Bean Clock

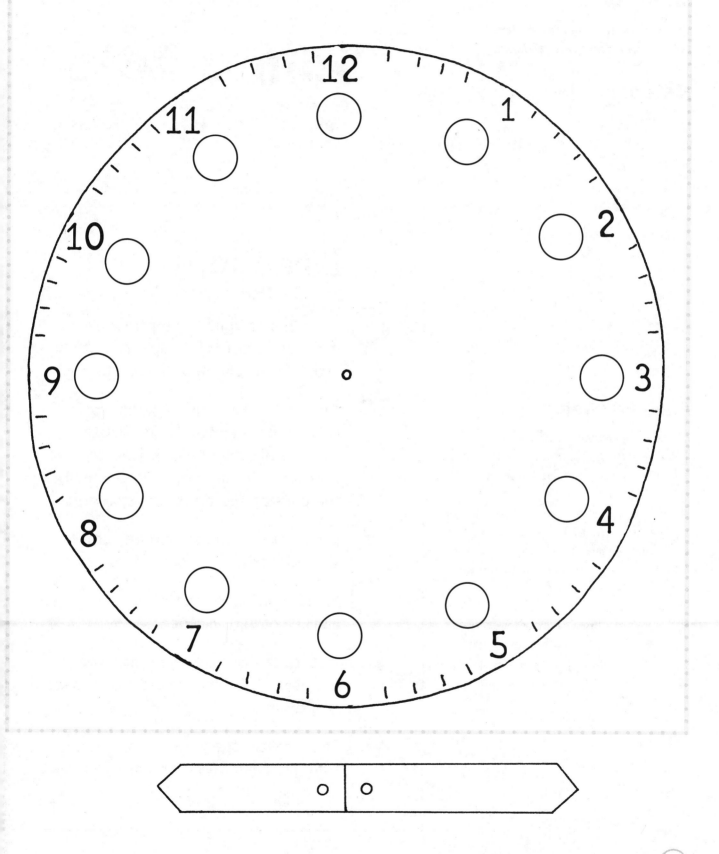

Spin a Date

Children count the number of days between two dates on a calendar.

Materials

* shoe box
* box label
* student directions
* scissors
* glue
* calendar (page 71)
* spinners (page 72)
* crayons or markers
* paper clips
* pencils
* teddy bear counters
* paper

Shoe Box Setup

Copy the calendar and spinners onto sturdy paper. Fill in the current month and dates on the calendar. Color the spinners. Laminate all the pieces. Place the calendar, spinners, paper clips, pencils, teddy bear counters, and paper in the shoe box. Glue the label to one end of the box and the student directions to the inside of the lid.

TIP Fill in a calendar for every month of the school year. Laminate the calendars, and you're ready to use this shoe box center year-round!

Counting Days

Spin a Date

Sunday   Monday   Tuesday

Directions
(for 2 or more players)

1. Use a pencil to hold the paper clip in the center of the 🎯 spinner. Spin the clip. Do the same with the ❋ spinner.

2. Put the two numbers together to make a one- or two-digit number. (If you spin a 1 and a 6, your number is 16.) If your number is larger than the ones on the calendar, spin again.

3. Put a marker on that number on the calendar.

4. Spin the spinners again. Put a marker on that number.

5. Count the days between the two numbers. Write the number on a sheet of paper.

6. Each player takes a turn. The player with the highest number wins that round.

Spin a Date

Month _____

Sunday	Monday	Tuesday	Wednesday	Thursday	Friday	Saturday

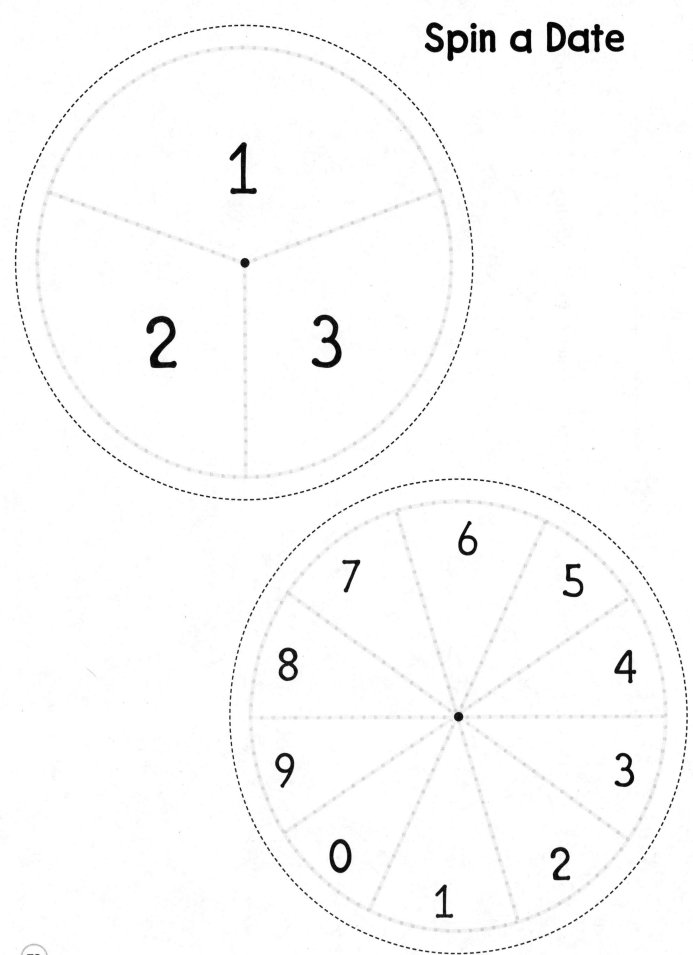

Spin a Date

Candy Shop

Children count coins to pay for candy.

Materials

- shoe box
- box label
- student directions
- scissors
- glue
- game board (page 74)
- candy cards (page 75)
- 50 pennies and 8 nickels (real or plastic)
- two resealable plastic bags

Shoe Box Setup

Copy the game board and candy cards onto sturdy paper. Color, cut out, and laminate all the pieces. Place the candy cards in one resealable bag and the coins in the other. Place the game board, cards, and coins in the shoe box. Glue the label to one end of the box and the student directions to the inside of the lid.

TIP Encourage children to "trade up" pennies to nickels as they count coins to pay for their candy. Challenge them to make their purchases with as few coins as possible.

Counting Money

Candy Shop

Directions

(for 2 players)

(1) Choose five or six pieces of candy to buy. Place the candy cards next to the cash register.

(2) Count out the money for each piece of candy. Place the coins on the counter to pay.

(3) Ask your partner to check to make sure you paid the right amount of money.

(4) Take turns being the shopper and the cashier.

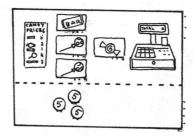

Candy Shop

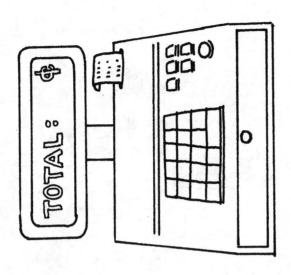

TOTAL: ¢

Counter

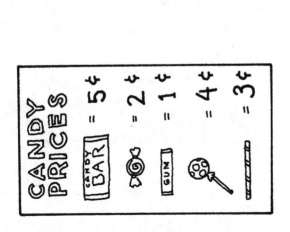

CANDY PRICES

CANDY BAR	= 5¢
	= 2¢
GUM	= 1¢
	= 4¢
	= 3¢

Candy Shop

In My Piggy Bank

Children count coins onto their piggy banks and then find the value of the coins.

Materials

- shoe box
- box label
- student directions
- scissors
- glue
- piggy bank pattern and coin strips (page 77)
- 5 nickels and 12 pennies (real or plastic; stored in a resealable bag)

Shoe Box Setup

Copy the piggy bank and coin strips onto sturdy paper. Color, cut out, and laminate all the pieces. Cut the slits in the piggy bank. Thread a coin strip through the slits. Place the piggy bank, coin strips, and coins in the shoe box. Glue the label to one end of the box and the student directions to the inside of the lid.

TIP Challenge students to find other ways to combine coins to make the same amount. For example, instead of six pennies and one nickel, they can use one penny and two nickels.

Counting Money

In My Piggy Bank

Directions

(1) Slide a coin strip up or down until a coin combination shows on the piggy bank.

(2) Count the coins onto the bank.

(3) Add to find the value of the coins in your bank.

(4) Ask a classmate to check your answer.

(5) Play again. Use a new coin strip.

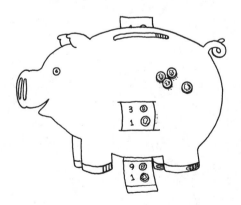

In My Piggy Bank

- - - - -

- - - - -

More Easy-to-Make Shoe Box Learning Centers

Add to your supply of shoe box centers periodically by creating fresh activities to keep student interest strong. Following are more ideas for making shoe box centers that reinforce counting skills. For each, use the reproducible templates (right) to make a label and write student directions. Glue the label to the outside of the box and the student directions to the inside of the lid.

Theme Chart

Children practice counting and data analysis skills as they roll a cube to complete a chart and then find the column with the most objects.

Make several three-column charts and laminate for durability. Stock the shoe box with the charts, a number cube (see page 15), and themed counters (such as crayons, paper clips, and erasers for a school theme). To play, have students place a different counter on each of the three headings on the chart. Children take turns rolling the cube three times and placing the corresponding number of counters in each column. After five rounds (or any other number of rounds), players count and write the number of objects in each column. Have players compare their totals in each column to see how close they are.

Directions

Sensory Shape Sort

Children explore attributes as they sort shapes by counting the number of sides on each.

Make a shape board by dividing a sheet of paper into four boxes. Label the boxes with the numbers 3, 4, 5, and 6, as shown. Cut out various shapes from sandpaper with three, four, five, and six sides. Make several variations of each shape. The shapes should be proportionate to one another in size, and they should each fit comfortably in the shape board boxes. Place the shape boards, shapes, and crayons in the shoe box. Have children choose a shape, count the sides, place it under the correct box, and make a rubbing. They can repeat this to make a rubbing of at least one shape per box.

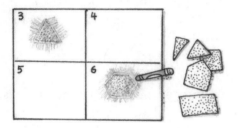

Counting on Names

Children sort names by number of letters to reinforce counting skills.

Write the numerals 1 through [the number of letters in the longest first name of students in the class] in bright colors on labels and affix to paper lunch bags (one per bag). Represent each numeral with the corresponding number of stickers. (If desired, include matching number words, too.) Write each student's name on an index card. Place bags and name cards in the shoe box. Have students sort the names by number of letters, placing them in the corresponding bags. When they are finished sorting, have them examine each bag's contents to learn more. For example, which bag has the most name cards? The fewest? Are there any bags with no name cards? How many bags have fewer than five name cards? Five or more? Students can make predictions first, and then count the cards in each bag to find out.

Sticker Slap

In this fast-paced game, children strengthen counting strategies to be the first to identify the card with the most stickers.

Make a set of game cards by placing one to ten (or any other range) small stickers on index cards. (You can also use a stamper or print out cards using small pictures from a clip art program.) Place the cards in the shoe box. To play, have two or more children shuffle the cards and divide them equally. (Depending on how many children are playing, they may set aside any extra cards.) Have children stack their cards facedown and on the count of three turn over the top card. The first player to slap the card with the most stickers takes that round of cards. If two or more cards have the same number of stickers, the first child to slap one takes the round. If children agree that it's a tie, that round can be set aside or children can play another round on top of the first and the winner of that takes all. Children play until they've turned over all the cards in their deck. For more counting, children can see who has the most cards at the end of the game.

Milk Jug Lid Toss

Children practice using tally marks to count as they experiment to see which way a milk jug lid lands when tossed 25 times.

Make a record sheet by dividing a sheet of paper into two columns. Label one column "Top Side Up." Label the other column "Top Side Down." Place a milk jug lid, copies of the record sheet, and pencils in a shoe box. Have children toss the milk jug lid 25 times, use tally marks to record the tosses, and count to see which way the lid landed most often. (Students can make a prediction first.)

Rectangle Race

This counting game lets children practice counting as they color in corresponding numbers of squares on a game board.

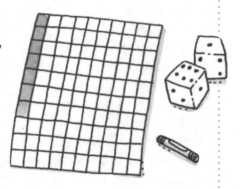

For this shoe box center, you'll need grid paper (about 10 by 10), crayons, and two dotted number cubes (page 16). To play, have each child take a sheet of grid paper. Children take turns rolling the number cubes and counting the total number of dots. They color in this many squares on their grid. Children take turns until one colors in the entire grid. The final roll needs to provide the exact number of squares needed. If the roll is too high, the next player takes a turn.

Checkered Boards

Children count and compare the colored squares on checkered boards to learn more about number relationships.

Create several checkered boards using one-inch grid paper. Color the squares on the grid paper using at least two colors for each board. You may color some boards in patterns (such as red, blue, red, blue) or randomly. Children may enjoy helping to make these boards. To use this center, have children choose a board and one of the colors on the board. Have children place a pom-pom (or other marker) on each square that matches that color. Children count the pom-poms and record the color and number. They can take the pom-poms off the board and repeat these steps for each color on the board. You may want to plan ahead and provide pom-poms in colors that match those on the boards. Have children compare the number of pom-poms they count for each color. To connect counting with measurement, students who are ready for a challenge can count the squares and compute to find the perimeter and area of the checkered boards.